STAR WARS

LIGHTSABER BATTLES

Written by Lauren Nesworthy

Project Editor Lauren Nesworthy
Project Art Editor Jon Hall
Senior Designer Clive Savage
Pre-production Producer Siu Yin Chan
Senior Producer Mary Slater
Managing Editor Sadie Smith
Managing Art Editor Vicky Short
Publisher Julie Ferris
Art Director Lisa Lanzarini
Publishing Director Simon Beecroft

Reading Consultant Linda B. Gambrell, Ph.D

For Lucasfilm
Assistant Editor Samantha Holland
Art Director Troy Alders
Story Group James Waugh, Pablo Hidalgo, and Leland Chee
Image Unit Tim Mapp and Nicole Lancoursiere

First American Edition, 2018
Published in the United States by DK Publishing
345 Hudson Street, New York, New York 10014

Page design copyright © 2018 Dorling Kindersley Limited
DK, a Division of Penguin Random House LLC
18 19 20 21 22 10 9 8 7 6 5 4 3 2 1
001–305825–Jan/2018

A catalog record for this book is available from the Library of Congress.

ISBN: 978-1-4654-6758-4 (Paperback)
ISBN: 978-1-4654-6759-1 (Hardcover)

DK books are available at special discounts when purchased in bulk for sales promotions,
premiums, fund-raising, or educational use. For details, contact:
DK Publishing Special Markets, 345 Hudson Street, New York, New York 10014
SpecialSales@dk.com

Printed and bound in China

A WORLD OF IDEAS:
SEE ALL THERE IS TO KNOW

www.dk.com
www.starwars.com

Contents

What is a lightsaber?

The lightsaber is one of the most ancient and rare weapons in the galaxy. They are used by beings who are connected to a powerful energy called the Force. Lightsabers are used like swords, with blades made from energy. They can slice through any material and block any attack!

Every lightsaber is powered by one of the mysterious kyber crystals.

How Does A Lightsaber Work?

Each lightsaber is made up of many different parts. Take a closer look inside to find out what a lightsaber needs in order to work.

The controls are used to adjust the blade's power or length.

The kyber crystal focuses energy and powers the weapon.

The blade emitter keeps the shape of the blade as it beams out.

The main hilt is where the energy for the blade is created.

The lightsaber's blade is weightless, but a Jedi warrior still needs strength to control the weapon.

Jedi and Sith

The galaxy is protected by warriors called the Jedi. They use the light side of the Force. Their lightsabers are usually green or blue.

Sith use the dark side of the Force. They fight with anger and hatred. Their lightsabers are red. The Jedi and Sith have fought in lightsaber duels for many years.

LIGHTSABER COMBAT

There are many ways of fighting with a lightsaber. Each Force user usually has one preferred "form." Here are a few examples.

Shii-Cho (shih-EE-choe)
The basic moves, learned by every lightsaber user.

Makashi (muh-KAA-shee)
Strike in a careful and controlled way, instead of using power and strength.

Soresu (sor-EE-soo)

Focus more on defending yourself, rather than attacking your opponent.

Ataru (uh-TAR-oo)

Use acrobatic jumps, twirls, and twists to beat your opponent.

Shien (shee-ENN)

Use your lightsaber to attack and block opponents. It takes a lot of strength!

Lightsaber lessons

All Jedi must learn the ways of the Force, and how to fight with a lightsaber. Usually, Jedi begin their training at a very young age. They are known as "younglings."

Younglings learn to use lightsabers with their eyes covered. This helps them practice Force-sensitivity. As they grow more advanced in their training, they become known as "Padawans."

HOW TO GET A KYBER CRYSTAL

Ezra must take a test in a Jedi temple. If he passes, he will be rewarded with a kyber crystal. This means that he is ready to become a true Jedi!

1. Ezra uses the Force to find a Jedi temple. He must "sense" the way.

2. He goes through a doorway where the walls are covered in ancient writing.

3. Ezra is tested by facing his fears. All Jedi must learn control.

4. It helps to listen to the wisdom of a great Jedi Master like Yoda.

5. Ezra passed! He can use the kyber crystal to build his own lightsaber.

A fierce battle

Qui-Gon Jinn falls in battle against Darth Maul. His Padawan, Obi-Wan Kenobi, bravely takes his place. Maul kicks Obi-Wan's lightsaber down a pipe. Just when it looks like all is lost, Obi-Wan uses the Force to summon Qui-Gon's lightsaber. It flies into Obi-Wan's hand, and with it he wins the duel!

Jedi Master Qui-Gon Jinn was not quick enough to defeat the evil Sith.

Dark side temptation

Jedi Anakin Skywalker has a duel
with a Sith Lord named Count
Dooku. He believes Dooku is
holding Senator Palpatine prisoner.

Anakin defeats Dooku by taking
his lightsaber. Palpatine then tricks
Anakin into killing Dooku. This is
not the Jedi way, but Anakin obeys.
Palpatine uses Anakin's anger to
lure him to the dark side.

Four-armed foe

The cyborg General Grievous battles Obi-Wan with a lightsaber in each of his four hands! The Jedi must use fast reflexes to block and dodge each blow at top speed.

Obi-Wan manages to use his own lightsaber to slice off two of the cyborg's hands. This makes it a slightly fairer fight!

Grievous has two green lightsabers and two blue lightsabers.

WHAT ELSE CAN YOU DO WITH A LIGHTSABER?

Lightsabers aren't just used in duels. These weapons can come in handy during all sorts of sticky situations!

The Grand Inquisitor throws his lightsaber at Ezra Bridger. This knocks the Padawan off a platform.

Kanan Jarrus destroys the controls of a door with his lightsaber to keep the Imperials out.

Obi-Wan Kenobi uses his lightsaber to block the shots from Jango Fett's blaster.

Luminara Unduli creates a doorway by cutting a hole in a solid wall with her lightsaber.

Luke Skywalker is held captive in a wampa's cave. He cuts himself free from the ice with his lightsaber.

Small but powerful

After years of secretly plotting
to take over the galaxy, Palpatine
reveals that he is Darth Sidious.
His terrible plans lead to him
battling Yoda. These two masters of
the Force clash in a fierce duel. Yoda
may be small, but he can do quick
jumps and backflips. These skills
help him in this dangerous fight.

The evil Sith Lord Darth Sidious will
not rest until all the Jedi are destroyed.

Friends to enemies

Anakin turns to the dark side.
His Master, Obi-Wan, must face
him in a deadly duel on a
fiery planet called Mustafar.
They have fought side by side for
many years, so they know each
other's best moves. Eventually,
Obi-Wan gets the better of
Anakin and defeats him with
one final blow.

A rebel victory

A rebel named Kanan Jarrus battles the Grand Inquisitor on a Star Destroyer. He is furious when the Inquisitor wounds his Padawan, Ezra. This drives the Jedi to fight with Ezra's lightsaber as well as his own.

Kanan becomes stronger in the Force than he has ever been before. He shatters the Inquisitor's double-bladed lightsaber!

TWO VERSUS ONE

Every Jedi can fight one-on-one.
However, all Jedi also know how
important it is to work together.
When it comes to fighting the Sith,
two is always better than one!

QUI-GON JINN
OBI-WAN KENOBI
VS.
DARTH MAUL

Darth Maul fights with a double-bladed
lightsaber. Qui-Gon Jinn and Obi-Wan
Kenobi tackle one blade each!

OBI-WAN KENOBI ANAKIN SKYWALKER VS. COUNT DOOKU

Obi-Wan Kenobi and Anakin Skywalker always work best side by side. A rescue mission leads to a duel with Count Dooku.

KANAN JARRUS EZRA BRIDGER VS. THE INQUISITOR

The Grand Inquisitor is a very skilled fighter. Kanan and Ezra rely on each other to get through every battle against him.

Fearless fighter

Ahsoka Tano can fight with two
lightsabers instead of one. When
she is on a mission for the Rebellion,
two Inquisitors try to capture her.

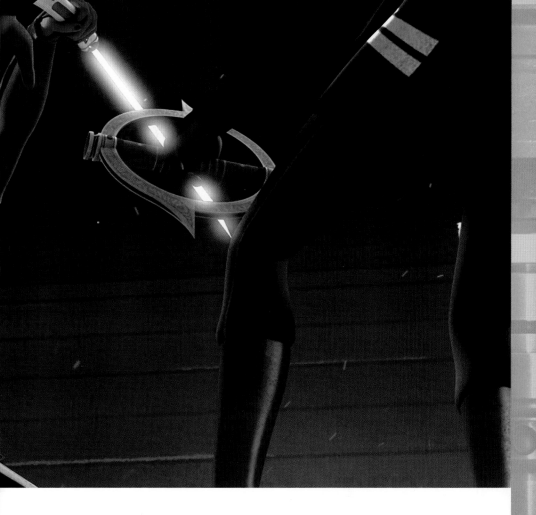

She must fight both of them at the same time! Ahsoka's amazing skills and quick reflexes help her to defeat them in battle.

Ahsoka's lightsaber blades are white.

A tragic reunion

Ahsoka takes on the evil Sith
Lord Darth Vader in a duel.
She destroys part of his mask with
her lightsaber. This reveals his face.

Ahsoka is heartbroken when she realizes that Vader is actually her old Jedi Master, Anakin Skywalker. The man who she once looked up to is now her enemy.

Father against son

Luke Skywalker is destined to save the galaxy from the evil Sith. To do this, he must battle against Darth Vader.

Their first duel takes place on a platform that hangs over a dangerously high drop! Vader's experience helps him defeat Luke. He then reveals a dark secret. He is Luke's father!

The brave traitor

Finn does not use the Force, but he is able to use a lightsaber. Finn and his friend Rey are attacked by Kylo Ren. When Kylo hurts Rey, Finn bravely fights back against the First Order warrior. However, his lightsaber skills are no match for Kylo's. Finn is injured badly in the duel.

Finn uses a lightsaber that once belonged to Luke Skywalker.

Forest fight

Rey may not have had any lightsaber training, but her connection to the Force makes her a strong fighter.

Rey first uses a lightsaber in a battle with Kylo Ren, in the snowy forest on Starkiller Base. Kylo is shocked by how skilled she is!

ONE-OF-A-KIND WEAPON

Every lightsaber in the galaxy is unique. However, there are some that are a little more unusual than others!

MACE WINDU'S LIGHTSABER

Jedi Master Mace Windu is the only Force user in the galaxy to wield a purple lightsaber.

EZRA BRIDGER'S LIGHTSABER

Ezra combines his lightsaber with a blaster. This means that he can switch between shooting at and dueling with his opponents!

THE INQUISITOR'S LIGHTSABER

Inquisitors are armed with double-bladed lightsabers. They throw these spinning weapons at their opponents—and they rarely miss!

AHSOKA'S LIGHTSABERS

After the Clone Wars, Ahsoka Tano fights with two lightsabers instead of one. Their white color shows that she is no longer in the Jedi Order.

Quiz

1. Who are the protectors of the galaxy?

2. What color is a Sith's lightsaber?

3. Which lightsaber form involves doing acrobatic jumps?

4. Which Jedi takes Qui-Gon Jinn's place in the duel against Darth Maul?

5. How many lightsabers does General Grievous fight with?

6. Which creature holds Luke Skywalker prisoner in its cave?

7. Where does a Padawan undergo the test to become a Jedi?

8. Which Sith Lord was once Ahsoka Tano's old Jedi Master?

9. Where does Rey battle against Kylo Ren?

10. Which Jedi Master has a purple lightsaber?

Answers on page 47

Glossary

cyborg
Someone who is part living and part robot.

dodge
To duck or to avoid something.

duels
Battles fought between two people.

the Force
An energy that flows through the galaxy.

Force-sensitivity
The ability of a person to detect or feel the Force.

heartbroken
Very saddened or distressed.

hilt
The handle of a weapon.

injured
Hurt or wounded.

Jedi
A group of warriors who defend peace and justice in the galaxy.

lure
To tempt someone, often with the promise of a reward.

plotting
Organizing or making a plan in secret.

reunion
To meet a person again.

shatters
Breaks apart into pieces.

Sith
A group of evil beings who use the dark side of the Force.

Index

Answers to the quiz on pages 44 and 45:
1. The Jedi 2. Red 3. Ataru 4. Obi-Wan Kenobi
5. Four 6. A wampa 7. In a Jedi temple 8. Darth Vader
9. The forest on Starkiller Base 10. Mace Windu

A LEVEL FOR EVERY READER

This book is a part of an exciting four-level reading series to support children in developing the habit of reading widely for both pleasure and information. Each book is designed to develop a child's reading skills, fluency, grammar awareness, and comprehension in order to build confidence and enjoyment when reading.

Ready for a Level 2 (Beginning to Read) book
A child should:
- be able to recognize a bank of common words quickly and be able to blend sounds together to make some words.
- be familiar with using beginner letter sounds and context clues to figure out unfamiliar words.
- sometimes correct his/her reading if it doesn't look right or make sense.
- be aware of the need for a slight pause at commas and a longer one at periods.

A valuable and shared reading experience
For many children, reading requires much effort, but adult participation can make reading both fun and easier. Here are a few tips on how to use this book with a young reader:

Check out the contents together:
- read about the book on the back cover and talk about the contents page to help heighten interest and expectation.
- discuss new or difficult words.
- chat about labels, annotations, and pictures.

Support the reader:
- give the book to the young reader to turn the pages.
- where necessary, encourage longer words to be broken into syllables, sound out each one, and then flow the syllables together; ask him/her to reread the sentence to check the meaning.
- encourage the reader to vary her/his voice as she/he reads; demonstrate how to do this if helpful.

Talk at the end of each book, or after every few pages:
- ask questions about the text and the meaning of the words used—this helps develop comprehension skills.
- read the quiz at the end of the book and encourage the reader to answer the questions, if necessary, by turning back to the relevant pages to find the answers.

Series consultant, Dr. Linda Gambrell, Distinguished Professor of Education at Clemson University, has served as President of the National Reading Conference, the College Reading Association, and the International Reading Association.